I0558998

KNOW NO STUDIES

HARIS VITALAKI

Paperback: 978-1-969919-00-8
eBook: 978-1-969919-01-5
Library of Congress Control Number: 2025921092

This is a work of fiction.

Ordering Information:

Prime Seven Media
518 Landmann St.
Tomah City, WI 54660

Printed in the United States of America

TABLE OF CONTENTS

EPISODE 1

Start the lesson?
-leave the lesson
Why leave?
- So we live
- So be it!!
No be back
-what if not

No More talk
-no more teach?
No More Learn
-no!!! More Learn
-Learn all
Then simply stop!
- the endless talk!!
-of the teacher !!!

Of the mind
-is there a stopping line?
-how find?
No starting point, no stopping line
-then no medals for athletes to find?
-so much difficult to try
-mean unite?

**Yes medals for
all to find!!**
-Me the gold you
the white?
-Me the ocean you the sky!!
Me the crown you the eye!!
-Me the eye say bye!!
-bye better bye!!

EPISODE 2

SAVE WATER

Learn again
-What again?
Planet
-our planet?
-Must plan
-save water
-I am thirsty
-I am dirty

Else?
-Air
-We breathe !!
Take a sip in through
the nose
!!!!!!!
Out through the toes
-how strange a thought
-easier to plant an oak!!
-easier to save the
world
This is why we
have this talk

-welcome heroes to help as all
-robbin hood can come along
-and pour some poor to show
the road
-to say the words
-to speak the truth!!
From the heart
-to the heart
-great plan!!
-we had enough!!
OK relax !!

7

EPISODE 3

EPISODE 4

So this is the time of the year..
  -This is the time of the ear?
  -This is the time not to hear!!!
No this is the time of the
  year to hear...
    -Heart!
    -Mind!
-Soul!
  -Music let's play
    -shake it babe.....
-everybody dance now

Music later now everybody
        listen to me...
-Who do you think you are???
-Yeah who does she think she is ?
-Who do they think they are?
          -Who am I?
      -I will tell you!
            -how know?
    -Me know everything

Enough!!!
-what?
You are Enough!
-are we Enough?
More than enough just
  as you are!
    - nice
    -no try?
Trust!!!

EPISODE 5

good morning
-good Morning Miss!!
Good...day
-do we pray?
-God Jesus
-Holly spirit
-wine spirit

-oh!! party spirit!
-yea!! lose control
-Lose lesson
lesson now!!
-Holly cow!!
I teach!
-you wish!!!!

Of any sort
-Cold
-hunger
-have a bit all!
**All the children
in the world**
-all the Chicken
in the world
**all the creature
in the world
All beings**
-bees?
Everything that is
-then is for all
That's all

Wish that...!
-Me start!!
-Me have all enough
-Me do art
-Me be smart
-Me eat much
Free from junk!!!
-Free from fear
-Pain

19

EPISODE 6

Who starts kids?
-who...stops miss?
Your phones please!!
-that's out of speak!
-out of question!
I have a suggestion!

What if we stop the
mobile application
-God bless the free nation!!
-followers extermination!!
-Influencers alienation
-cosmic complication!!

-stars full of frustration
-the end of civilisations!!!!
-Atmospheres suffocation!!!
What a lovely conversation!!!
-Oh no total disorientation
Just keep the application
Text around the nation!!
-Milliion word affirmation!

-endless gaming with no limitation!!
-Listen to music with devoted
concentration!
Searching for no
motivation, just enjoy
the sensation
-Enjoy the creation!!!
Of all that's all!!

EPISODE 7

Good morning kids
-Good morning miss dear!!
Time to think !!
what brought you here??
-My mother brought me here!!

-My mothers brought me here
Mother earth has sealed the deal!!
-We must study if that is clear!!
Study?? what would rather hear?
-Music wraps the atmosphere
- gives us passion, stops the fear!!

Fear of
-what if something goes wrong
- difficult to fix the world
-what if I lose my home
Trust that you are not alone
- show me how to be strong
First accept the feeling tone
-and if the test fails the score?
-how to bare the mother's moan?
-if pain strikes on its own?

Turn inward let go
-close your eyes and calm the soul
-why bother after all
-I chose for my world
-my mind is my own
-hear me shout that I'm whole!!!
Then it's time for you to go!!

EPISODE 8

Hello kids!
-yellow miss?
colours for you to think!!
-I chose the pink
-I chose the blue of the sea
-I'd rather have a golden shield
-shield of light no-one can see!
-it will only be for me!
-keep me safe when I need
  -Now bullies won't be pleased!
   And what will they might think?
    -hey? I can't control my fist
  -the wind swivels it against my teeth!!

-Then simply think
-chose to do the right thing
-respect my life and the other leaving being!
-everything in my universe will only be working for me!!
-What a lovely thing
-and be the being I was meant to be!!
-I don't know what to be!!

Follow the path easier for you to see
 - darkness no more stopping me
 -my wellbeing my priority
 -my power will come from within
 And win
  -what?
   Your right to be free
    You are free

31

EPISODE 9

35

EPISODE 10

Hello today!!
-It's time for break!
-the ice?
**Antarctica must
survive**
-white bears where
will lie?
-igloos only history
reminds?
**Eskimos t-shirt not
yet designed!!!**
-penguins where will spend
their time

-ice ice baby need to
change the rhymes!!
-Music industry would go
through hard times
Just leave the ice
-let me freeze behind
my eyes

-beneath my skin
-against my will
- still
-just breathe
And think
-that's it...
I'm done
- I'm back
-start from
the ashes

-lift the figure up
-there is so much more to ask
- ask
-do ...did.....done

Was that...the bell rang?
-are we safe..can we run?
Run

39

EPISODE 11

Now quiet!! Need to begin
-I am quiet for you to be pleased
Otherwise how be?
-I lost my ability to think
-To choose
-to live
-never did

Never lived?
-not that easy as it seems
-only follow your wish
-everything already fixed
-try constantly to fit
How would you rather be?
-me relaxed upon the scene
-so much stress should never be
- mind can't take other beat
-why not just change it
-teaching style

-Feel like swimming in the Nile
-please aware of the crocodile
-of the current
-of the stream
-I need to scream!!

And I think I need to think
-Or just stop and simply be
- something is happening within?
-tingling is covering my skin
-My head
-My teeth

-all I feel is all I need
-I am a winner I shall win
-I am a liver I shall live!!
I am so proud of you kids!!

www.ingramcontent.com/pod-product-compliance
Lightning Source LLC
Chambersburg PA
CBHW040849120626
46547CB00001B/90